Learning AngularJS the Easy Wa
by Brendon Co

ISBN-13: 978-1495947940
ISBN-10: 1495947947

Cover Image by Brendon Co

About the Author

Brendon Co is a programmer and entrepreneur who has a passion for JavaScript programming language. He's the creator and lead developer of Movie R Us internet video streaming for mobile devices and the lead developer on many web-based, mobile and desktop development projects.

Acknowledgements

I'd like to take this opportunity to thank everyone who made this book possible. It was a tremendous amount of work, and I appreciate all the help and guidance that I received along the way.

I would like to thank my family and friends for supporting me and encouraging me throughout the years.

Introduction

Why AngularJS?

HTML is great for declaring static document but falters when we try to use for declaring dynamic views in web application. AngularJS let you extend HTML vocabulary for your application. The result will make your tags more readable, expressive and quick to develop.

Alternatives

Other frameworks deal with HTML by either abstracting away HTML, CSS and JavaScript or by providing an imperative way for manipulating the DOM. Neither of these address the problem that HTML was not designed for dynamic views.

Extensibility

AngularJS is a toolset for building the framework most suited to your application development. It is fully extensible and works well with other libraries. Every feature can be modified or replaced to suit your unique development workflow and feature needs.

Using Code Examples

This book is here to help you get your job done. In general, you may use the code in this book in your programs and documentation.

I appreciate, but do not require, attribution. An attribution usually includes the tittle, author, publisher, and ISBN. For example: "*Learning AngularJS the Easy Way* by Brendon Co"

Chapter 1. The Basics

Include AngularJS library in html file. E.g. index.html

```
<script
src="https://ajax.googleapis.com/ajax/libs/angularjs/1.2.10/angular.min.js></scrip
t>
```

To tell AngularJS to be active in this portion of the page. In this case the entire document. Add ng-app beside html tag.

```
<html ng-app>
```

Link form and models. This means that any changes to the control update the data in your model, and when you change the model it updates the control.

```
<input type="text" ng-model="yourName" placeholder="Enter a name here">
```

The {{ }} are a declarative way of specifying data binding locations in the HTML. AngularJS will automatically update this text whenever the yourName property changes.

```
<h1>Hello {{yourName}}!</h1>
```

Try it! Type in the control and see it update.

```
<!doctype html>
<html ng-app>
  <head>
    <script src="https://ajax.googleapis.com/ajax/libs/angularjs/1.2.10/angular.min.js"></script>
  </head>
  <body>
    <div>
      <label>Name:</label>
      <input type="text" ng-model="yourName" placeholder="Enter a name here">
      <hr>
      <h1>Hello {{yourName}}!</h1>
    </div>
  </body>
</html>
```

Output

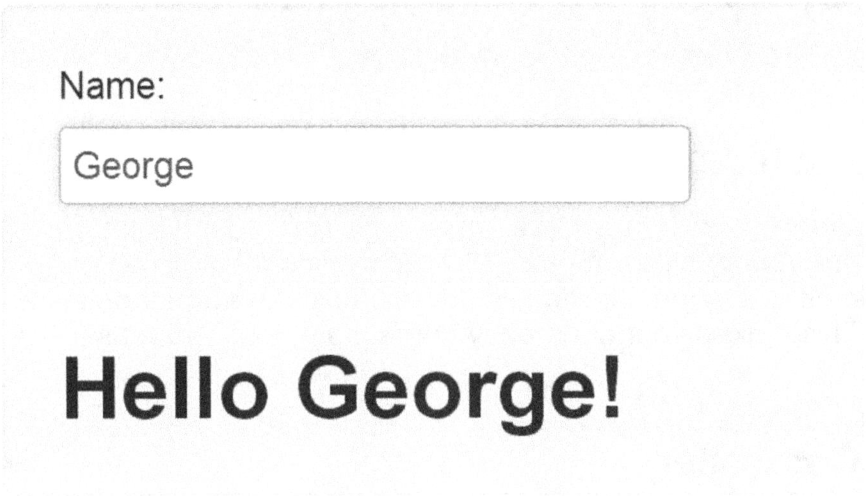
Name:
George
Hello George!

Chapter 2. Add Some Control

Plain JavaScript

Unlike other frameworks, there is no need to inherit from proprietary types in order to wrap the model in accessors methods. Angular models are plain old JavaScript objects. This makes your code easy to maintain, test and reuse.

Controller

Controllers are the behavior behind the DOM elements. AngularJS let you express the behavior in a clean readable form without the usual in updating the DOM, registering callbacks or watching model changes.

It's very simple to declare a controller, add ng-controller in an element e.g. div. The behavior of content under this element will be managed using the TodoCtrl class defined in todo.js.

```
<div ng-controller="TodoCtrl">
```

The controller is the code behind the view. There is no DOM manipulation or framework specific. Just simple, readable JavaScript.

$scope contains your model data. It is the glue between the controller and the view. The $scope is just one of the services that can be injected into the controller. You can define your own model name e.g. todos, addTodo, remaining or archive.

We are creating the model with two initial todo items. Notice that you simply assign your model to the $scope and AngularJS reflects the state in the UI automatically. The model data is a Plain-Old-JavaScript-Object no need to wrap it in proxy or accesses the property through special setter methods.

```
function TodoCtrl($scope) {
  $scope.todos = [
    {text:'learn angular', done:true},
    {text:'build an angular app', done:false}];
```

$scope.addTodo We are assigning the behavior into the $scope so that the ng-submit can invoke it.
ng-submit Enables binding angular expressions to onsubmit events.
Additionally it prevents the default action (which for form means sending the request to the server and reloading the current page) but only if the form does not contain an action attribute.

```
$scope.addTodo = function() {
  $scope.todos.push({text:$scope.todoText, done:false});
  $scope.todoText = '';
};
```

$scope.remaining This is a computed property. No need to define its dependencies or worry about when it needs to be updated.

```
$scope.remaining = function() {

  var count = 0;

  angular.forEach($scope.todos, function(todo) {

    count += todo.done ? 0 : 1;

  });

  return count;

};
```

$scope.todos = [ ] You can replace the model with new instance at any time, without doing any special model listener registration.

Try the complete sample code below.

index.html

```
<!doctype html>
<html ng-app>
  <head>
    <script src="https://ajax.googleapis.com/ajax/libs/angularjs/1.2.10/angular.min.js"></script>
    <script src="todo.js"></script>
    <link rel="stylesheet" href="todo.css">
  </head>
  <body>
    <h2>Todo</h2>
    <div ng-controller="TodoCtrl">
      <span>{{remaining()}} of {{todos.length}} remaining</span>
      [ <a href="" ng-click="archive()">archive</a> ]
      <ul class="unstyled">
        <li ng-repeat="todo in todos">
          <input type="checkbox" ng-model="todo.done">
          <span class="done-{{todo.done}}">{{todo.text}}</span>
        </li>
      </ul>
      <form ng-submit="addTodo()">
        <input type="text" ng-model="todoText"  size="30"
               placeholder="add new todo here">
```

```
          <input class="btn-primary" type="submit" value="add">
        </form>
      </div>
    </body>
  </html>
```

todo.js

```
function TodoCtrl($scope) {
  $scope.todos = [
    {text:'learn angular', done:true},
    {text:'build an angular app', done:false}];

  $scope.addTodo = function() {
    $scope.todos.push({text:$scope.todoText, done:false});
    $scope.todoText = '';
  };

  $scope.remaining = function() {
    var count = 0;
    angular.forEach($scope.todos, function(todo) {
      count += todo.done ? 0 : 1;
    });
    return count;
  };
```

```

    $scope.archive = function() {
      var oldTodos = $scope.todos;
      $scope.todos = [];
      angular.forEach(oldTodos, function(todo) {
        if (!todo.done) $scope.todos.push(todo);
      });
    };
  }
```

todo.css

```
  .done-true {
    text-decoration: line-through;
    color: grey;
  }
```

Output

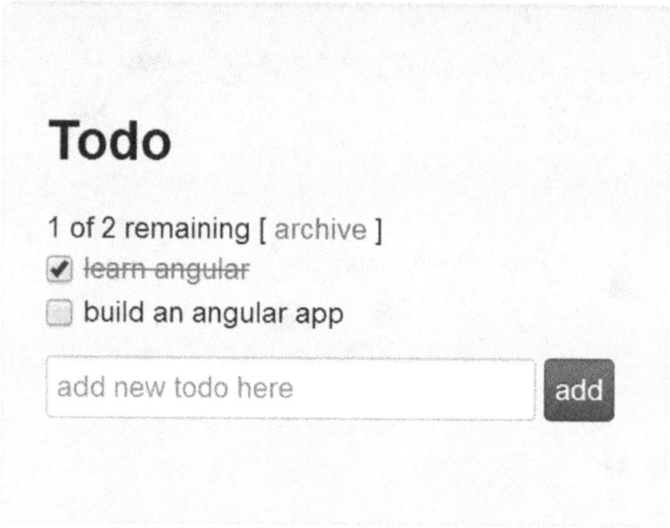
Todo
1 of 2 remaining [archive]
learn angular
build an angular app
add new todo here
add

Chapter 3. Create Reusable Components

Directives

Directives is a unique and powerful feature available only in Angular. Directives let you invent new HTML syntax, specific to your application.

Reusable Components

We use directives to create reusable components. A components allow you to hide complex DOM structure, CSS, and behavior. This lets you focus either on what the application does or how the application looks separately.

Localization

An important part of serious application is localization. Angular's locale aware filters and stemming directives give you building blocks to make your application available in all locales.
Let's create our own iframe component.

1. Use the module's directive() method to define new HTML vocabulary for our components.
2. Define <my-iframe> component.
3. The restrict specifies the HTML format of the component. In this case the <my-iframe> must be an HTML element.
4. The templateUrl is the HTML which needs to be rendered by the browser instead of the <my-iframe> placeholder. Inside this HTML, we can have other directives within it. For now, let's keep it simple.

5. scope.$watch The scope provide API ($watch) to observe model mutations. Meaning, if there 's something change in the attrs.iframeSrc, the ($watch) function will be triggered. Hence, it will render the src assigned to the element src attribute.

component.js

```
angular.module('components', [])
  .directive('myIframe', function() {
   return {
     restrict: 'E',
     link: function(scope, element, attrs) {
       scope.$watch(attrs.iframeSrc, function(value){
         if(value){
           element.attr('src', value);
         }
       });
     },
     templateUrl: 'template/my-iframe.html',
     replace: true
   };
})
```

template/my-iframe.html

```
<iframe width="100%" height="100%"></iframe>
```

In index.html, add the directive <my-iframe>.

```
<div>
   <my-iframe iframe-src="mySrc"></my-iframe>
</div>
```

app.js

The app module declares a dependency on the components module, which ensures that the directives in the components module are also loaded into the application.

```
angular.module('app', ['components'])

.controller('FrameController', function($scope) {
  $scope.mySrc = “https://www.w3.org”;
});
```

```
angular.module('app', ['components'])

  controller('FrameController', function($scope) {

    $scope.mySrc = “https://www.w3.org”;

});
```

Try the complete sample code below.

index.html

```
<!doctype html>
<html ng-app="app">
  <head>
    <script src="https://ajax.googleapis.com/ajax/libs/angularjs/1.2.10/angular.min.js">
    </script>
    <script src="components.js"></script>
    <script src="app.js"></script>
</head>
  <body>
    <div ng-controller="FrameController">
      <div><my-iframe iframe-src="mySrc"></my-iframe></div>
    </div>
</body>
</html>
```

app.js

```
angular.module('app', ['components'])

.controller('FrameController', function($scope) {
  $scope.mySrc = "https://www.w3.org";
});
```

components.js

```
angular.module('app', [])

.directive('myIframe', function() {
  return {
      restrict : 'E',
      link : function (scope, element, attrs){
         scope.$watch(attrs.iframeSrc, function(value){
             if(value){
                 element.attr('src', value);
             }
         });
      },
      templateUrl : 'template/my-iframe.html',
      replace : true
};
});
```

template/my-iframe.html

```
<iframe width="100%" height="100%"></iframe>
```

How to use Transclude?

Let's say that we want to pass in an entire template rather than a string or an object. And create a dialog box component. The dialog box should be able to wrap any arbitrary content.

To do this, we need to use the transclude option.

index.html

```
<!doctype html>
<html ng-app="transcludeDirective">
  <head>
    <script src="http://code.angularjs.org/1.2.10/angular.min.js"></scrip
t>
    <script src="script.js"></script>
  </head>
  <body>
    <div ng-controller="Ctrl">
      <my-dialog>Check out the contents, {{name}}!</my-dialog>
    </div>
  </body>
</html>
```

my-dialog.html

ng-transclude means that the directive that marks the insertion point for the transcluded DOM of the nearest parent directive that uses transclusion.
Any existing content of the element that this directive is placed on will be removed before the transcluded content is inserted.

```
<div class="alert" ng-transclude>
</div>
```

script.js

```
angular.module('transcludeDirective', [])
  .controller('Ctrl', function($scope) {
    $scope.name = 'George';
  })
  .directive('myDialog', function() {
    return {
      restrict: 'E',
      transclude: true,
      templateUrl: 'my-dialog.html'
    };
  });
```

Output

Check out the contents, George!

Chapter 4. Intercept HTTP Response

AngularJS has created interceptors to allow you to intercept responses from the server e.g. error responses (HTTP status codes 300 and up).

When working with security filter on the server end of your application, sometime your session may time out resulting in a 401 unauthorized response. The simplest to do is just have the client side application either reload the page or show a friendly message or redirect to a login page.

See below sample code that will call GET on api/data.json .

```
var App = angular.module('myapp', []);

App.controller('myController', function ($scope, $http, $timeout) {
   $scope.data = [];
   function update(successCallback, errorCallback) {
      $http.get("api/data.json").success(function(data, status) {
         successCallback (data);
      }).error(function(data, status){
         errorCallback();
      });
   }

   function errorCallback () {
     $timeout(update, 3000);
   }

   function successCallback(data){
     $scope.data = data;
     $timeout(update, 3000);
   }

   update();
}
```

Now we setup an interceptor by calling config on the App object and adding the interceptor to the injected $httpProvider.

$httpProvider – Allows to configure http headers to all requests.

The interceptors are service factories that are registered with the $httpProvider by adding them to the $httpProvider.interceptors array. The factory is called and injected with dependencies (if specified) and returns the interceptor.

The response property of the returned object is for testing purposes. As it will only receive responses that fall below status 300, there is no use for it if we want to catch 401.

```
App.config(['$httpProvider', function ($httpProvider) {
    $httpProvider.interceptors.push(function ($q) {
        return {
            'response': function (response) {
                        // Do something on success
                return response || $q.when(response);
            },
            'responseError': function (rejection) {
                if(rejection.status === 401) {
                    location.reload();
                }
                return $q.reject(rejection);
            }
        };
    });
}]);
```

The responseError handler does not stop the program flow after the location.reload().

$q – A promise/deferred implementation inspired by Kris Kowal's Q. Composing ansynchronous promises in JavaScript.

To know more about CommonJS Promise, you can visit this link (http://wiki.commonjs.org/wiki/Promises).

Chapter 5. ng-repeat

The ngRepeat directive instantiates a template once per item from a collection. Each template instance gets it own scope, where the given loop variable is set to the current collection item, and $index is set to the item index or key.

This example initializes the scope to a list of names and then uses ngRepeat to display every person.

filter – A filter formats the value of an expression for display to the user. They can be used in view templates, controllers or services and it is easy to define your own filter.

To know more about filter (http://docs.angularjs.org/guide/filter).

$index – iterator offset of the repeated element (0..length-1).

To know more about ngRepeat (http://docs.angularjs.org/api/ng.directive:ngRepeat).

index.html

```
<!doctype html>
<html ng-app>
 <head>
   <script src="http://code.angularjs.org/1.2.10/angular.min.js"></script>
   <script src="http://code.angularjs.org/1.2.10/angular-animate.min.js">
   </script>
 </head>
 <body>
   <div ng-init="friends = [
     {name:'John', age:25, gender:'boy'},
     {name:'Jessie', age:30, gender:'girl'},
     {name:'Johanna', age:28, gender:'girl'},
     {name:'Joy', age:15, gender:'girl'},
     {name:'Mary', age:28, gender:'girl'},
     {name:'Peter', age:95, gender:'boy'},
     {name:'Sebastian', age:50, gender:'boy'},
     {name:'Erika', age:27, gender:'girl'},
     {name:'Patrick', age:40, gender:'boy'},
     {name:'Samantha', age:60, gender:'girl'}
   ]">
     I have {{friends.length}} friends. They are:
```

```
      <input type="search" ng-model="q" placeholder="filter friends..." />
      <ul class="example-animate-container">
        <li class="animate-repeat" ng-repeat="friend in friends | filter:q">
          [{{$index + 1}}] {{friend.name}} who is {{friend.age}} years old.
        </li>
      </ul>
    </div>
  </body>
</html>
```

animate.css

```
.example-animate-container {
  background:white;
  border:1px solid black;
  list-style:none;
  margin:0;
  padding:0 10px;
}

.animate-repeat {
  line-height:40px;
  list-style:none;
  box-sizing:border-box;
}

.animate-repeat.ng-move,
.animate-repeat.ng-enter,
.animate-repeat.ng-leave {
  -webkit-transition:all linear 0.5s;
  transition:all linear 0.5s;
}

```

```
.animate-repeat.ng-leave.ng-leave-active,
.animate-repeat.ng-move,
.animate-repeat.ng-enter {
  opacity:0;
  max-height:0;
}

.animate-repeat.ng-leave,
.animate-repeat.ng-move.ng-move-active,
.animate-repeat.ng-enter.ng-enter-active {
  opacity:1;
  max-height:40px;
}
```

Output

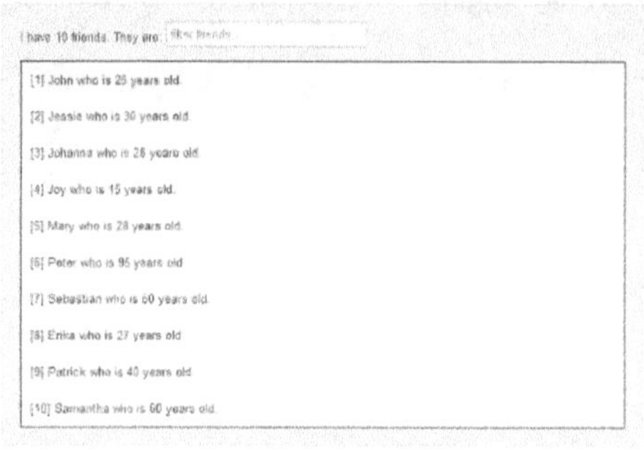
I have 10 friends. They are:
[1] John who is 25 years old.
[2] Jessie who is 30 years old.
[3] Johanna who is 28 years old.
[4] Joy who is 15 years old.
[5] Mary who is 28 years old.
[6] Peter who is 95 years old
[7] Sebastian who is 50 years old.
[8] Erika who is 27 years old
[9] Patrick who is 40 years old
[10] Samantha who is 60 years old.

Chapter 6. Service

What are Angular Services?

Angular services are singletons objects or function that carry out specific tasks common to web applications. Angular has a number of built-in services, such as $http service, which provide access to the browser's XMLHttpRequest object for making requests to a server. Like other Angular variables and identifiers, the built-in services always start with $ (such as $http mentioned above). You can also create your own custom services.

Using a built-in service $http

The $http service is a function which takes a single argument – a configuration object – that is used to generate an HTTP request and returns a promise with two $http specific methods: success and error.

```
$http({method: 'GET', url: '/someUrl'}).
  success(function(data, status, headers, config) {
    // this callback will be called asynchronously
    // when the response is available
  }).
  error(function(data, status, headers, config) {
    // called asynchronously if an error occurs
    // or server returns response with an error status.
  });
```

Since the returned value of calling the $http function is a promise, you can also use then method to register callbacks, and these callbacks will receive a single argument – an object representing the response.

A response status code between 200 and 299 is considered a success status and will result in the success callback being called. Note that if the response is a redirect, XMLHttpRequest will transparently follow it, meaning that the error callback will not be called for such responses.

Creating a Custom Service

To create a custom service is very easy.

hello.js

```
angular.module('app').factory('helloFactory', function(){
   return {
      sayHello: function(text){
         return "Factory says \"Hello " + text + "\"";
      }
   };
});
```

Using a Service

To use an Angular service, you identify it as a dependency for the component (controller, service, filter or directive) that depends on the service. Angular's dependency injection subsystem takes care of the rest. The Angular injector subsystem is in charge of service instantiation, resolution of dependencies and provision of dependencies to components as requested.

Angular injects dependencies using constructor-injection. The dependency is passed to the component's factory/constructor function. Because JavaScript is a dynamic typed language, Angular's dependency injection subsystem cannot use static types to identify service dependencies. For this reason a component must, explicitly, define its dependencies by using one of the injection annotation methods.

⚠ **Constructor – Injection** – The basic idea with constructor-injection is that the object has no defaults and instead you have a single constructor where all of the collaborators and values need to be supplied before you can instantiate the object.

Constructor-Injection enforces the order of initialization and prevents circular dependencies.

Dependency Injection – is a software design pattern that allows the removal of hard-coded dependencies and makes it possible to change them, whether at run-time or compile-time.

Injecting Service into Controller

In above hello.js JavaScript, add a controller function called HelloCtrl. In the controller, specify your service to use, in this case our helloFactory. Let's define a scope helloFactory to be displayed in the html.

```
angular.module("app", []);

angular.module('app').controller("HelloCtrl", ["$scope", "helloFactory",
function($scope, helloFactory){
   $scope.helloFactory = helloFactory.sayHello("World");
}]);
```

index.html

```
<!doctype html>
<html ng-app="app">
   <head>
      <title>Hello World</title>
   </head>
   <body>
      <div ng-controller="HelloCtrl">
         <p>{{helloFactory}}</p>
      </div>


      <script
src="https://ajax.googleapis.com/ajax/libs/angularjs/1.2.10/angular.min.js"></scri
pt>

      <script src="js/hello.js"></script>
   </body>
</html>
```

Output

Factory says "Hello World"

Chapter 7. Basic Routing

Angular provide two features to map routes onto a templates that get rendered inside of the view. These features are ngRoute and ngView directives.

What is ngRoute?

The ngRoute module provides routing and deeplinking services and directives for your app.

What is ngView?

ngView is a directive that complements the $route service by including the rendered template of the current route into the main layout. Every time the current route changes, the included view changes with it according to the configuration of $route service.
Dependency: ngRoute module.
First we create our main page. Specify ng-app to auto-bootstrap an AngularJS application. Add ng-view directive to where you want to display a template of your page. Angular will insert the view into the index.html page were ng-view directive was identified. Oh, you need angular-route in order the routing to work. That's it for the main page

index.html

```
<!doctype html>
<html ng-app="app">
  <head>
    <title>Hello World</title>
  </head>
  <body>
    <div>
      <a href="#/home">Home</a>|
      <a href="#/helloWorld">Hello World</a>
      <div>
        <div ng-view></div>
       </div>
    </div>

    <script
src="http://code.angularjs.org/1.2.10/angular.min.js"></script>
    <script src="http://code.angularjs.org/1.2.10/angular-
route.min.js"></script>

    <script src="js/hello.js"></script>
  </body>
</html>
```

Now let's create two simple templates called home.html and helloworld.html. You can design this page to look fancy using CSS. For now, let's keep it simple.

home.html

```
<div>{{defaultPage}}</div>
```

helloworld.html

```
<div>{{hello}}</div>
```

Load ngRoute module.

```
angular.module("app", ["ngRoute"]);

angular.module("app").config(["$routeProvider",
function($routeProvider) {
   $routeProvider.when('/helloWorld', {templateUrl:
"pages/helloworld.html", controller:"app.HelloWorldController",
controllerAs: "helloworldpage"});
   $routeProvider.when('/home', {templateUrl: "pages/home.html",
controller:"app.HomePageController", controllerAs: "homepage"});
   $routeProvider.otherwise({redirectTo: "/home"});
}]);
```

⚠ **$routeProvider** – Used for configuring routes.

when(path, route)

Adds a new route definition to the $route service.

otherwise(params)

Sets route definition that will be used on route change when no other route definition is matched.

Define a controllers called “app.HelloWorldController” and “app.HomePageController”. These controllers will display a simple text in our templates (home.html or helloworld.html).
Below is the full hello.js source code.

hello.js

```
angular.module("app", ["ngRoute"]);

angular.module("app").config(["$routeProvider",
function($routeProvider) {
   $routeProvider.when('/helloWorld', {templateUrl:
"pages/helloworld.html", controller:"app.HelloWorldController",
controllerAs: "helloworldpage"});
   $routeProvider.when('/home', {templateUrl: "pages/home.html",
controller:"app.HomePageController", controllerAs: "homepage"});
   $routeProvider.otherwise({redirectTo: "/home"});
}]);

angular.module("app").controller("app.HelloWorldController", ["$scope",
function($scope){
   $scope.hello = "Hello World!";
}]);

angular.module("app").controller("app.HomePageController", ["$scope",
function($scope){
   $scope.defaultPage = "Home Page";
}]);
```

Chapter 8. Unit Test

Overview

This chapter will guide you through installation of all the tools you need to run automated tests using Selenium, and Protractor.

Protractor

Protractor is an end to end test framework for AngularJS applications built on top of WebDriverJS. Protractor runs test against your application running in a real browser, interacting with it as a user would.
Protractor can be run as standalone binary, or included into your tests as library. Use Protractor as a library if you would like to manage WebDriver.

⚠ **WebDriver** is a tool for automating testing web applications, and in particular to verify that the web application work as expected. It aims to provide friendly API that's easy to explore and understand, which will help make your tests easier to read and maintain.

WebDriverJS Supported Browsers

WebDriverJS is supported in the following browsers:

- IE 8+

- Firefox 10+
- Chrome 12+
- Opera 12+
- Android 4.0+

Setting up the environment

Install protractor with.

```
npm install -g protractor
```

(Or omit –g if you'd prefer not to install globally).
The example test expects a selenium standalone server to be running at localhost port 4444. Protractor comes with a script to help download and install the standalone server. Run below command line to download or update the webdriver manager.

```
webdriver-manager update
```

This installs selenium standalone server and chrome driver to protractor/selenium. Start the server with below command line.

```
webdriver-manager start
```

Create a protractor configuration file called "protractor.conf.js".

The configuration file tells Protractor what tests to run, how to connect to a webdriver server, and various other options for reporting.
Below is what protractor.conf.js configuration file looks like.

```
// protractor.conf.js

exports.config = {

  seleniumServerJar: 'lib/selenium/selenium-server-standalone-2.39.0.jar',

  chromeDriver: 'lib/chromedriver',

  seleniumAddress: 'http://localhost:4444/wd/hub',

  specs: ['unit-test/protractor/e2e/*.js'],

  capabilities: {

    browserName: 'chrome',

    version: '',

    platform: 'ANY'

  }

}
```

The configuration file must specify a way to connect to webdriver. This can be

- seleniumAddress – The address of a running selenium standalone server.

- seleniumServerJar – The location of the selenium standalone .jar file on your machine. Protractor will use this to start up the selenium server.
- sauceUser and sauceKey – The username and key for SauceLabs account. Protractor will use this to run test on SauceLabs.

Writing a tests

By default, Protractor uses Jasmine as its test scaffolding. Protractor exposes several global variables.

- browser – this is the wrapper around an instance of webdriver. Used for navigation and page-wide information.
- element – is a helper function for finding and interacting with elements on the page you are testing.
- by – is a collection of element locator strategies. For example, elements can be found by CSS selector, by ID, or by the attribute they are bound to with ng-model.
- protractor – is the protractor namespace which wraps the webdriver namespace. This contains static variables and classes, such as protractor.Key which enumerates the codes for special keyboard signals.

In Chapter 7, I talk about Basic Routing. Let's use this as an example to create a simple test case.
Create the test file and call it "hello-spec.js". Save and place in this location "unit-test/protractor/e2e/" as specified in the protractor.config.js file. The example below is a basic test on which it will check whether the binding property "defaultPage" has the expected value, in this case the expected value is "Home Page".

hello-spec.js

```
describe('hello world message app.HomePageController', function() {

 beforeEach(function(){
  // Load the Application homepage.

  browser.get('http://localhost/angularjs/index.html');

 });

 describe('Define ($)scope.defaultPage ->', function() {

  it('should show hello world message', function() {

   // Find the element with binding matching 'defaultPage' - this will

   // find the <div>{{defaultPage}}</div> element.

   var pageName = element(by.binding('defaultPage'));

   // Assert that the text element has the expected value.

   // Protractor patches 'expect' to understand promises.

   expect(pageName.getText()).toEqual('Home Page');

  });
```

```
  });

});
```

Type in the command line below to run the test script. Protractor takes one argument which is a configuration file.

```
protractor test_dir/protractor_dir/protractor.conf.js
```

Output

```
Using the selenium server at http://localhost:4444/wd/hub

hello world message app.HomePageController

   Define ($)scope.defaultPage ->
      should show hello world message

Finished in 1.268 seconds
1 test, 1 assertion, 0 failures
```

If we want a style to be mandatory, we can define in the test script. To do that, add a test script and define the class name to check. In our case, let's call the class name "popup-style". When the test script is run, it will throw an exception, that you need to define the "popup-style" class in your home.html file or add a property called popupStyle property in your scope, define the value as "popup-style".

```
describe('Mandatory popup-style class ->', function() {
  it('should define a popup-style class', function() {
    element(by.css('.popup-style')).getText().then(function(className) {
      var classNameStyle = $('.popup-style').getText();
      expect(classNameStyle).toEqual(className);
    });
  });
});
```

Run the test script again. Since we haven't define the class name in our home.html file or in controller, it will throw an exception.

```
protractor test_dir/protractor_dir/protractor.conf.js
```

Output

```
Using the selenium server at http://localhost:4444/wd/hub

hello world message app.HomePageController

  Define ($)scope.defaultPage ->
    should show hello world message

  Mandatory popup-style class ->
    should define a popup-style class

Failures:

 1) hello world message app.HomePageController Mandatory popup-style class
-> s
hould define a popup-style class
  Message:
   NoSuchElementError: no such element
```

Visit **Protractor** API documentation website to understand how to write Protractor tests.

URL: https://github.com/angular/protractor/blob/master/docs/getting-started.md

Refer to Chapter 7 Basic Routing. Modify home.html and define the directive ngClass with the scope called “popupStyle”. In “hello.js”, modify “app.HomePageController”. Add a scope “popupStyle” with value “popup-style”.

hello.js

```
angular.module("app").controller("app.HomePageController", ["$scope",
function($scope){
            $scope.defaultPage = "Home Page";
            $scope.popupStyle = "popup-style";
}]);
```

home.html

```
<div ng-class="popupStyle">{{defaultPage}}</div>
```

Run the test script.

```
protractor test_dir/protractor_dir/protractor.conf.js
```

Output

```
Using the selenium server at http://localhost:4444/wd/hub

hello world message app.HomePageController

  Define ($)scope.defaultPage ->
    should show hello world message

  Mandatory popup-style class ->
    should define a popup-style class

Finished in 2.217 seconds
2 tests, 2 assertions, 0 failures
```

Learning AngularJS the Easy Way

Brendon Co

Revision History

2014 – 03- 17	First release

www.ingramcontent.com/pod-product-compliance
Lightning Source LLC
LaVergne TN
LVHW052316060326
832902LV00021B/3918
* 9 7 8 1 4 9 5 9 4 7 9 4 0 *